Strategic Position in Strategic Management

by

Poornima Madushani Patabendige

The Copyright Act prohibits (subject to certain very limited exceptions) the making of copies of any copyrighted work or of a substantial part of such a work, including any unauthorized use, distributing, reproducing or similar process. The Publisher may be liable to criminal prosecution and civil claims for the damages caused. Written permission to make a copy or copies must therefore normally be obtained from the publisher (Nerdynaut.com) in advance. It is advisable also to consult the publisher if in any doubt as to the legality of any copying which is to be undertaken.

Copyright © 2018 Nerdynaut. All Rights Reserved.

Title: Strategic Position in Strategic Management
Publisher: Nerdynaut
Author: Poornima Madushani Patabendige
Publication Date: December 26, 2018
Edition: 1.0
ISBN: 9781792708695
Cover credit: Designed by Nerdynaut/Freepik.com

Table of Contents

1.0 Introduction 1
2.0 External environment analysis 5
   2.1 Macro environment and the PESTEL analysis 5
      2.1.1 Political 6
      2.1.2 Economic 7
      2.1.3 Social 8
      2.1.4 Technological 10
      2.1.5 Environmental factors 11
      2.1.6 Legal 11
   2.2 Industry level and the five-force analysis 12
      2.2.1 Intensity of the rivalry 13
      2.2.2 Threat of new entrance 14
      2.2.3 Bargaining power of the suppliers 15
      2.2.4 Bargaining power of the buyers 16
      2.2.5 Threats of substitutes 16
   2.3 Competitors and the markets and the strategic group analysis 17
3.0 Internal environment 19
4.0 Summary 20

1.0 Introduction

In simple terms strategic management is all about managing the strategy. Strategic management looks at three main areas. They are as follows.

1. Strategic position
2. Strategic choice
3. Strategy in action

The strategic position usually looks at the impact on the strategy of four things naming external environment, strategic capabilities of the organization including the resources and the competences of the organization, expectations of the stakeholders and the culture of the organization.

Strategic choice involves in the generation of the strategic options, careful evaluation of those options and finally choosing the most suitable strategy for the organization.

Strategy in action is mainly focusing on the implementation of the most suitable strategy.

strartegic position	startegic choices	startegy into action
external environment strategic capabilities stakeholder expectations culture	developing the startegic options careful evaluation of those options choosing the most suitable startegy.	changes need to be done to the culture structure leadership etc

In this book, we are going to cover the concept of the strategic position in strategic management.

As mentioned above the strategic position mainly focuses on the impact on the strategy of the

- External environment
- Strategic capabilities including the resources and the competences
- Expectations of the stakeholders
- And finally, the culture

To understand the strategic position we need to undertake a strategic analysis which in turn gives an idea about the changes in the environment and the opportunities that we can gain out of those changes, the resource base of the organization and how it is going to yield us sustainable competitive advantages, stakeholders and their expectation and how does the culture make impacts on the performance of the organization.

In the strategic analysis, we need to do an external and internal analysis and the external analysis is usually done to understand the environment which is outside to the organization whereas the internal analysis is undertaken to understand the environment which is predictable and locates inside the organization. in the external environment, there are mainly 3 layers of the external environment naming

- Macro environment
- Industry or sector
- Competitors and markets

To do the macro environmental analysis, an analysis called PESTEL analysis has to be undertaken whereas 5 force analysis is done to analyse the industry or the sector and strategic group analysis to analyse the competitors and the markets.

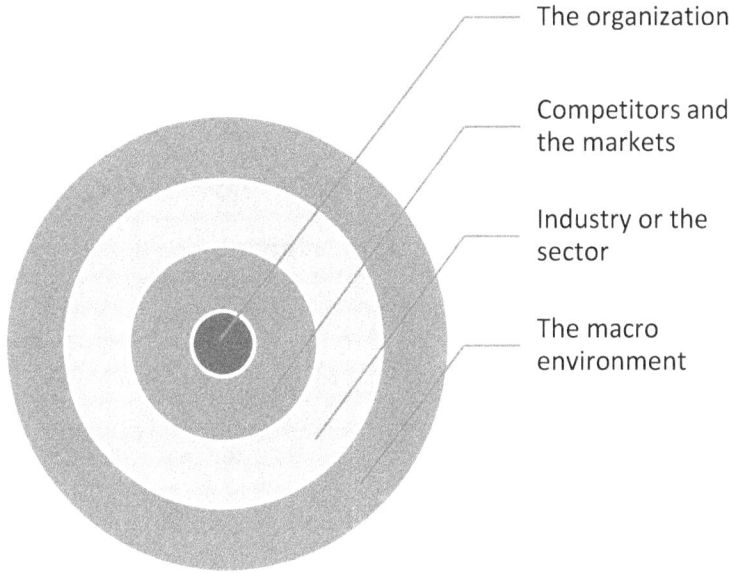

2.0 External environment analysis

2.1 Macro environment and the PESTEL analysis

The macro environment is coming under the external environment and it is out of the control of the organization. And these macro environmental factors affect the performance of the organization in two ways. Either favourably or adversely. And the extent of the impact of the factors on the organizations differs from one organization to another or one industry to another.

PESTEL framework stands for;

    P - Political

    E - Economic

    S - Social

    T - Technology

    E - Environmental

    L – Legal

2.1.1 Political

This refers to the extent to which the government policies may affect the organization. For an example, the government could impose a new **tax policy** to a particular industry and hence all the organizations in that particular industry will have to pay the tax as per the new regulation suggests. Because of that their revenue is shrunk since they need to pay taxes on the revenue they earn in case if the new tax system has increased the tax rate.

Government stability also coming under the political environment and when we are doing the macro environmental analysis, we need to take that into account too. For an example, recently Sri Lankan political situation was worse and as a result of that huge amount of investments were taken out of the country. That instability status of the political status made adverse impacts on the business organizations.

Trade regulation is again one of the ways in which the government makes impacts on the organizations and this would make impacts in either way.

2.1.2 Economic

This refers to the direction of the economy of the particular country which in turn has implications on the performances of the organizations. For an example factors such as **GNP trends, inflation, exchange rates, unemployment rates** are some of the examples coming under the economic environment.

In practice when a particular country is operating at a higher inflation rate, the business organizations have to do their pricing by considering the inflation rate of that particular country in order for them to cover up their costs and to make sure that they achieve their target profits as well. On the other hand, when the inflation rate of the particular country is relatively high the purchasing power of the consumers are less. So, when the organizations do their pricing decisions based on the inflation rates, they need to take into account that as well.

When a country is facing a continuous depreciation of the domestic currency that also affects the organization's performances. Mostly the importers have to pay more.

Because of that their purchasing costs are relatively high. But such depreciation in the domestic currency will yield higher cash flows to the exporters.

When the unemployment rate is higher, it is an implication that most of the people of the particular country are unemployed. As a consequence, their purchasing power may be less. When we are making pricing decisions, we need to consider these factors as well.

2.1.3 Social

This environment includes factors such as **demographics, changes in lifestyles, social trends and education levels of the consumers**. These factors have direct impacts on the organizations in terms of buying patterns of the customers.

For an example, in the seasons the sales of the organizations increase and that is coming under these social factors. At the same time when the ageing population of the country is relatively high then it yields opportunities to organizations to extend their businesses which accommodate the ageing population. Likewise, when the population of the country is educated their buying habit is related to a rational. They are not just buying what is available in the market. Instead, before they are making the decision to buy the product, they think whether this product is inlying with our requirements, whether this product is produced in an environmentally friendly way etc. Likewise, they are not just buying what they are offered but they think whether this product is worth what they pay. Because of that as a manager we need to make sure we have addressed all the requirements of the customer unless they won't buy what we produce and will definitely switch to a competitor who caters all the requirements that they seek from a commodity.

2.1.4 Technological

And this environment includes the **rate of technological changes, technology transfer policy, government and industry spending on research and development**.

For an example when the production process is automated the efficiency, productivity can be increased and hence as an organization we can gain a competitive advantage by providing commodities at a lower price. But still, such an automation process requires a huge investment.

At the same time, this technological environment is subjected to rapid changes and this will quickly outdated the technology we use and will give the competitive advantages to the competitors who use the latest technology.

And these technological factors give implications whether to come up with a particular new product or not, whether to enter into a particular market or not, and whether to outsource some of the processes or not.

2.1.5 Environmental factors

Factors such as **environmental regulations, waste management and energy issues** are coming under this.

At the same time, ecological and environmental factors such as climate and the weather are also coming under this. Because the changes in the climate and the weather has direct impacts on certain industries such as farming, agriculture, tourism and insurance. And with the rise of the need for corporate social responsibility, the organizations have looked at things such as recycling procedures, waste disposal, carbon footprint and the sustainability too.

2.1.6 Legal

Employment laws, health and safety laws are considered under this. And there is an interrelation between the political and the legal factors whereas the political factors are imposed through the policies of the government and the legal factors should comply with those political factors. As organizations we always need to make sure that we comply with those laws otherwise we need to pay penalties in case we have not complied with them.

So, these are the factors we need to take into account in the macro level under the strategic analysis. In this PESTEL analysis, we need to identify all the factors in the macro level that have implications to our business and then we have to carefully select the key drivers which makes more impacts on the organizations to which we need to come up with strategies as managers mainly through building scenarios.

Now let's look at the factors we need to consider in the next level.

2.2 Industry level and the five-force analysis

The next level that we need to look at is the industry level and the respective analysis we need to undertake in this level is the five-force analysis. And this helps to measure the attractiveness of a particular industry or sector in terms of the competitive forces. According to Michael Porter, the followings are the competitive forces.

- The intensity of rivalry among established firms
- Risk of entry by potential competitors
- Bargaining power of the suppliers
- Bargaining power of the buyers

- The threat of the substitutes

2.2.1 Intensity of the rivalry

This measures the number of rivalry firms and the strength of the rivalry firms in the particular industry. That means here as managers we need to look at how many rivalry firms are operating in the industry and the strength that they possess over the industry. If they are offering high-quality products at a lower price than we offer, then we need to take measures in order to increase our product quality along with some price-cutting strategies. Otherwise, our customers will switch to those rivalry products and hence we will lose the market share we are currently possessing.

And when the number of rivalry firms is high and the strength that they possess over the market is much higher than we do, it is said that the attractiveness of the industry is less. And if we are already in the particular industry then we need to take measures in order to increase our competitiveness in terms of increasing our product quality and offering our products at a lower cost if possible. And even after that if it is not possible to cope up with the competitiveness then it is better to leave the particular industry.

2.2.2 Threat of new entrance

This refers to the extent to which the barriers to entry does exist in the industry. Lower the barriers higher the risk of our market share will be taken by a newly established business. Higher the barriers lower the risk. And this barriers to entry include the followings.

- Access to inputs
- Economies of scale
- Absolute cost advantages
- Well organized brands

As mentioned above when the particular industry has limited access to the required resources it is not that easy for a new business to come and establish a new business in that particular industry. Access to resources may be limited due to the regulations of the government such as patents and limited availability of the resources too.

When the economies of scales are existing in a particular industry then the cost of production of that industry is relatively cheaper and as a newcomer, we will not be able to compete with that lower prices. So that again we will not be able to enter into that particular industry.

When a specific industry has well-organized brands again the barriers to entry does come into existence.

2.2.3 Bargaining power of the suppliers

This measures the power that the suppliers have over the organization. when a specific company has more suppliers the control that the suppliers have over the organization is relatively lower. So that they cannot make impacts on the organization in terms of bargaining the prices. But when the organization has relatively a lower number of suppliers those suppliers will have the bargaining power over the organization and the specific organization will depend on the suppliers. The suppliers will provide supplies at a higher rate of prices which in turn will cause the business to increase the prices for them to achieve their targeted profits and that will lead the customers to switch to competitors products which are relatively cheaper.

2.2.4 Bargaining power of the buyers

This refers to the power of the consumers and the extent to which they can influence the pricing decisions of the organization and the quality of the products. The bargaining power of the organization is not measured in terms of the number of customers but by the number of sellers in the particular industry. When the number of sellers in the industry is relatively high the customers are capable of switching from one product to another product offered by different sellers. Because of that the business organization should make sure that the customers' requirements are addressed by the organization to the letter. Otherwise, they will switch to another competitor who produces the same product which gives a higher value than we offer. This will lose our prevailing profitability and also the long-term survival of the business too.

2.2.5 Threats of substitutes

When the substitutes are in the market then again, the likelihood of customers switching from one product to another is greater.

When these five factors are high the attractiveness of the industry is said to be lower and if you are a new business searching an industry to establish a new business then you should not go for that industry and if you are an organization already in that you better leave the organization or change it.

2.3 Competitors and the markets and the strategic group analysis

The next level in the external environment is the competitors and the market. To analyse this we need to carry out a strategic group analysis. This helps to recognize organizations which have the same strategic characteristics. The strategic group analysis can be done based on two or three characteristics and mostly by taking into accounts the followings.

- Product diversity
- Geographical coverage
- The range of distribution channels used
- Brands
- Marketing effort

- The degree of vertical integration
- Product quality
- Pricing policy etc.

And this strategic group analysis is useful in three ways.
1. When understanding the level of the competition.
2. When analysing the strategic opportunities.
3. When analysing the mobility of the barriers.

3.0 Internal environment

Under the internal environmental analysis what we are analyzing is the strategic capabilities of the organization and it includes the resources and the competences of the organization. strategic capabilities always refer to the capabilities of the organization which in turn yield long-term survival or competitive advantage. In this, the followings are considered.

- What are the strategic capabilities of the organization?
- The way that those strategic capabilities contribute towards the superior performances and the way those strategic capabilities yield competitive advantages to the organization. The way of recognizing strategic capabilities.
- The way of managing the development of strategic capabilities.

4.0 Summary

- In this book, we discussed that the strategic management has three main phases naming
    - Strategic positioning
    - Strategic choices
    - Strategy in action
- But here in this volume we mainly focused on the strategic positioning in which a strategic analysis needed to be carried out.
- And the strategic analysis involves in external and internal environmental analysis and the external environment analysis involves in PESTEL analysis for the macro environment, five force analysis for industry or the sector and finally a strategic group analysis for the competitors and the markets.

www.ingramcontent.com/pod-product-compliance
Lightning Source LLC
Chambersburg PA
CBHW071205220526
45468CB00003B/1170